D0550684

**NORFOLK
LIBRARIES & INFORMATION SERVICE**

881864

PETERS	19-Dec-01
JF	£4.99

Text copyright © 1996 Vic Parker
Illustrations copyright © 1996 Emily Bolam

The rights of Vic Parker and Emily Bolam to be identified
as the author and artist of the work have been asserted.

First published in 1996 by Hodder Children's Books,
a division of Hodder Headline plc,
338 Euston Road, London NW1 3BH.

All rights reserved

10 9 8 7 6 5 4 3

ISBN 0340 65675 1 Hardback
ISBN 0340 65676 X Paperback

A catalogue record for this book is available from the British Library

Printed in China

Bearobics

Emily Bolam
Vic Parker

Hodder
Children's
Books

A division of Hodder Headline plc

Deep in the forest there's a
thumping, bumping sound,
A drumming and a humming, a stomping on the ground.
The pumping rumpus rhythm takes control of both your feet
And suddenly you find yourself getting with the beat.
But where's that boogie coming from,
That rapping in the air?

Out of the beat box of one shaggy bear.

Come on everybody! Do that **wild Bearo**bics thing.

Let yourself go! Get into the S**wing**!

With a **fizzle** in their fingers and a **tingle** in their toes,

TWO kangaroos know how Bearobics goes.

Three giggling gorillas now get into the groove.

Bopping and shoowapping, just watch them move!

Going to a go-go, **four** ostriches arrive

To show off **fancy** footwork in the **jumping** jive.

With a stripy shoulder Shimmy, yelling out for more,

Five funky tigers fandango on the floor.

Do a hippy hippy shake to the left and to the right.

Seven cool penguins can't get enough.

With a *slide* to the *side* they strut their stuff.

Going even *faster* now - mustn't stop to rest,

Jumping in a jumble,
Eight bunnies bounce the best.

The pace is really pounding – get ready for high kicks.

Nine *flashy* frogs go crazy with their lively leggy tricks.

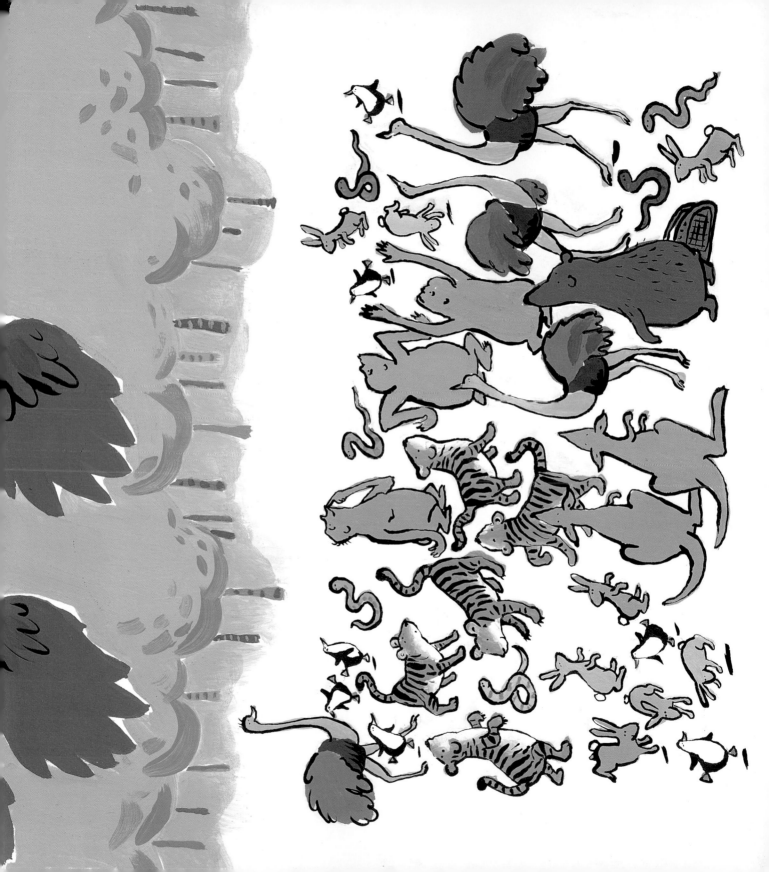

Ten dizzy mice disco in and seize the chance

To jitterbug and tango in the huge Bearobics dance.

Now the forest's buzzing with the great Bearobics beat. A Million ants come marching on a Billion stamping feet.

The air is hot and heavy with the **throbbing** all around,
Everyone is jamming to the wild Bearobics sound.

Once you try Bearobics, you'll never want to stop.
Just rap to this Bearobics beat and dance
until you drop.